Pearls 4 Girls

A Guide for Teens With Dreams

Darolyn D. Mangum

Pearls 4 Girls

A Guide for Teens With Dreams

Darolyn D. Mangum

Although the author and publisher have made every effort to ensure that the information in this book is correct at press time, the author and publisher do not assume and hereby disclaim any liability to any party for any loss, damage, or disruption caused by errors or omissions, whether such errors or omissions result from negligence, accident or any other cause.

Copyright © 2015 Developing Dreams Publishing

All rights reserved.

ISBN-10: 0990989003

ISBN-13: 978-0-9909890-0-4

Acknowledgments

As a girl growing up, I would always say, if I had girls, I wanted to be the best role model I could be. Being the mother of two wonderful girls, I searched for ways to help them become, strong, independent women. They grew up to be exactly what I prayed they would be, strong, successful, and independent. This book was written with the future of young girls in mind, who I hope will also become successful women.

This book would not be possible without the love and support of my husband, Richard, for allowing me to pursue my dreams. My daughters, Richelle and Richae', for giving me the best experience as a mother.

Throughout the years so many amazing girls and women have shared their stories and lives with me, for that I am grateful.

Lastly, a special thank you to my mother, Evelyn J. Tyler and my sister, Carlette Tyler Newman. Although both of you are no longer with me on earth, you are both a part of my daily thoughts and prayers. The strength and courage you both had surpasses what I could ever imagine. My sisters Kimberly A. Boyd and Sharon J. Gillins for all of your love and support.

Dedication

Dedicated to my daughters, Richelle and Richae', for making motherhood a breeze! I enjoyed every moment of our "girl time" and the many "girl talks" we had! Thank you both for being my best friends!

Introduction

Pearls for Girls: A Guide for Teens with Dreams

Sugar and Spice

The image of teen females has changed over the years due to the influence of social media, music, fashion, books, and television. Many of you may have heard the saying, "Sugar and spice and everything nice, that's what little girls are made of." When baby girls are born, the parents are showered with "ooh's," "aaaah's" and everything pink. Girl's, according to "grandma's golden rules," are supposed to be soft spoken, wear pretty dresses, frilly lace, bows in her hair, walk with her shoulders back and head high. You may have seen or been told of how girls in charm school walked with books on their heads to practice the "proper" way to walk. If you look at pictures of teen girls in older books, magazines, or television shows from the 70's, 80's, 90's (The Brady Bunch, The Cosby Show, It's a Different World, Full House, Fresh Prince, Saved by the Bell, Sister, Sister) you will notice that the mannerisms, conversations, and the way the girls dressed are much different from today. Of course, as years go by, styles change, society changes, and as you know…everything in your life changes, especially during those "glorious teen years."

As girls become teens, they often lose their "sugar" and become more "spice" while they try to find their identity and place in the world. Understanding your purpose is important. You were born with a unique personality, endless abilities, and multiple gifts. To live a happy, healthy, successful life, you must remember… life is built on choices you make, your choices determine your happiness, successes, or failures. One of the greatest challenges in life as a teen is deciding what to do with the things you can control. You have control over things such as your attitude, friends you choose, words you speak, things you listen to, what you read, and what you watch. Each of these things have the possibility to influence the choices you make. However, there are things in life you have no control over such as, who your parents are, your brothers and sisters, the color of your skin, your race, the shape of your body, the texture of your hair, or the color of your eyes.

How you feel about yourself determines how far you will go in life. You are a teen from 13-19, those six years are short in comparison to the length of time you spend as an adult. So when you find yourself anxious to become an adult, keep in mind that you should embrace your teen years because you will never get them back. Many of you have older sisters, friends, tv idols, etc. that you spend more time trying to fit in with the older crowd that you miss out on your teen years. Enjoy life, be yourself, and be happy with who and where you are! Life is full of surprises, opportunities, and disappointments.

Do you ever feel depressed, unhappy, or worthless? Do you feel pressure to look and be perfect for your friends, and the adults in your life? Are you supposed to look like the reality TV stars or skinny celebrities in magazines? Do you hang with people even though you know they are not good for you to be around?

If you answered yes to any of the questions above, this book is for you. This book was written to help you feel better about your teen years, love the skin you are in, guide you to discover your purpose, and find the answers to many of your questions. As you read, focus on being happy with who you are and who you were created to be. Each chapter will end with, "My Jewelry Box." As you may know, a jewelry box is a place where you put your jewelry to keep them in a secure place. In this book, "My Jewelry Box," is for you to journal "precious gems" (your thoughts or ah ha moments) you learned from the chapter. In chapter 10, you will see "My Treasure Chest," which is a series of questions for you to answer from each chapter in the book. Use the questions as a guide as you search for your key to happiness. If you answer them honestly, you can open your mind to see life as a teen differently. You will be on your way to discovering a new you. My hope is that everyone who reads this book will unlock their own treasure chest.

Let's get this journey started. Welcome to the beginning of the rest of your life.

Chapter 1

Free To Be Me

"Wanting to be someone else is a waste of the person you are."
—Marilyn Monroe

Loving who you are is the foundation for happiness and success in your life. You hold the key to change how you feel on the inside, regardless of how you think you look on the outside. Your inner beauty shines as you develop confidence, create your happiness, and discover self-love, all of which depends on your self-esteem. Self-esteem is having respect and confidence in yourself.

Your level of self-esteem depends on how much you value yourself, as well as what you think others think of you; self-esteem builds from the inside out. Rather than looking at your imperfections, mistakes, and focusing on things you do wrong, focus on your strengths or things you do well. There are many things that influence whether you have high or low self-esteem as you struggle to find your own identity. Some of those things are family relationships, status, opinions, and idols.

Family relationships are a huge influence, as a teen you begin to search for your own identity and want to break away from the way you are viewed in the eyes of your parents. In order to become your own person you may start acting out to prove that you are growing up and are no longer your parents" little princess." Acting out doesn't always mean being rebellious, you may act silly, become a people pleaser, or simply withdraw to become the invisible child and prefer to stay in your room alone. As a teen, in our home, I was the oldest of 3 girls. I had the responsibility of having more chores, helping my siblings with homework, and always being told that I had to set the example for my younger sisters. Being the oldest child may come with a lot of resentment because you may feel as though you are being an additional parent to your siblings. I remember the struggle of trying to find my identity, while being a role model for my sisters at the same time. Trying to do so made it difficult to find my place with my friends. Most teens want to have their own circle of friends and be a part of a group.

Status and which group you are a part of is important to many teens. It becomes important to buy designer clothes, be a popular cheerleader, the smart girl, party girl, athletic girl, bad girl, the rebel, or do things totally different to gain attention. When you become a part of a group you have to live up to it, after all you have earned your reputation…right? If you steer away from the group, you feel you will be judged.

The opinions of others matter as a teen. How you see yourself depends on what you believe others think about you. For instance, your family and friends may see you as a smart student because you have consistently been on the honor roll. You get a challenging class and receive a few low test grades. Once your friends start making comments about your low scores, you then start second guessing whether you are as smart as you thought. You were once your friends' academic idol, now you are feeling like an average student because of your friends opinions.

Idols influence teens, whether they are peers, athletes, musicians, or TV stars. Teens lose their identity by idolizing those they consider to have "great lives, bodies, money, beauty, popularity, etc." Many times idols can be negative influences yet the person that idolizes them can see no wrong in anything they say or do. Even if the idol goes to jail, gets caught with drugs, or any other negative behavior, they continue to get support from their fans. Rather than striving to be the best you, it's more trendy in your teen years to be a follower of someone who has already made a name for themselves.

> "I like having popular friends. It makes me feel cool and makes everybody want to be with our group. When we hang out and have parties, it's fun because we all like the same things. I want to keep the friends I have because if

> I don't have them I would be a nerd like some of the other people at my school."- Jennifer C.

If you continue trying to be someone you are not, you disappoint those who believe in you the most. Being yourself you are more likely to have people supporting you even when life gets tough, they believe in you because you are genuine. You must say to yourself, I am who I am. I do not need approval from anyone to be me. How you see yourself is what other people will see, so you determine what people think about you by the way you act. You build your reputation by your actions.

> **TIP**: Stop comparing yourself to others, surround yourself with positive people, and don't just think you are beautifully and wonderfully made…BELIEVE IT. Be free to be you. "Be yourself, everyone else is already taken."-Oscar Wilde

My Jewelry Box

_____

_____

_____

_____

_____

Chapter 2

Uniquely Me

Happy Girls are the prettiest.
—Audrey Hepburn

As a teenage girl, your body image affects your ability to feel confident. When you look in the mirror, you may focus on things you dislike. We can all find something that we would like to change about the way we look. When I was a teenage girl, I was very thin. Most of the girls had nice bodies, in my opinion, and I wanted to look like them. I was very unhappy with my weight. Standing in front of the mirror was not my favorite place. There were a group of boys that called me Olive Oyl, she was the girlfriend of an old cartoon character, "Popeye." I was so self conscience of my weight. I wore a size 0 in high school. (Imagine that: 0). Everyone was created to have their own look. Even if you look like your mother, father, sister, brother, grandmother, etc. there is still something unique about you. You must learn to look beyond what you see on the outside and focus on the inner you. The feelings you have on the inside reflect on the outside. Do you feel loved or unloved, joy or pain?

In order to focus on the inner you and not dread every time you look in the mirror, here are some things you can do, every morning and before going to bed. When you look in the mirror look into your eyes, not at any other part of your body and say, "I love every part of me," say it several times. The first time you say it, you may feel silly or not believe what you are saying because that pimple on your face, your unruly hair, or whatever you want to change, is reminding you of what you don't like. Look beyond that negative thought. In order to remember to do this, you may want to write, "I love every part of me," on a post it note, a small piece of paper, or be creative, decorate a piece of paper and put it in a small frame in your bathroom to remind you to say it. After repeating this each day, you will notice new thoughts and feelings about yourself. Repeat it as often as you want, it doesn't have to only be morning and before bed. The more you practice the quicker you will not dread looking in the mirror. This is a great way for you to see that you can control your thoughts and think positive about yourself, if not, the negative thoughts will always get in the way.

If you are very uncomfortable with your body, it may be difficult to look in the mirror because your thoughts affect your self-esteem. Even if what you think about yourself is not true, the more you focus on it, the more it seems real. For instance, someone can tell you, how pretty you are, you will think, "you must not see my fat cheeks, my big ears, my pudgy nose…" You see yourself differently than others, remember, "beauty is in the eyes of the beholder." That means we all see things differently, what you may think is beautiful someone else may not and vice versa.

> "Unique means being the only one of its kind, unlike anything else. It does not mean simply "unusual" or "rare." For example, something isn't "very unique," it's just unique. Something is either unique or not; therefore, "very unique" is meaningless. -Moriah L.

> **TIP**: Embrace who you are! What does being unique mean to you? You are UNIQUELY YOU!!!

My Jewelry Box

_____
_____
_____
_____
_____
_____

Chapter 3

Daughters vs. Mothers

"Mothers and daughters become closest, when daughters become mothers."— Unknown

Mother-daughter relationships change more than any other relationship in the home during teen years. Daughters are usually, "daddy's little girl," no matter how old they get. Especially during the teen years, most fathers let the mothers do the "girl stuff" as they often play the role of referee. At birth, your parents had to do what they knew to do in order to care for you. Unfortunately, babies don't come with instructions and crystal balls don't come with teenage girls.

When you were younger you probably had a great relationship with your mother, only to find as a teen the relationship changed. Or you may not have been close to your mom as a child, now you want a relationship with her more than ever, but you are not sure where to start. Maybe your biological mother has not been in your life, for various reasons, you may have had a mother-daughter relationship with another adult female. Whatever the situation may be, the next few years may be filled with up's and down's as you and your mother try to adjust to the changing reality of the "new" you. Your needs and wants regarding your relationship with adults in general are changing, especially with your mother. Although, there are some mothers and daughters who have no problems in their relationship during teen years. Does being a teen have to mean conflict?

It is difficult for some mothers to let go of their "baby girl" because she knows that it won't be long before her baby is an adult. Mothers want to give their daughters space to grow and hold on to them at the same time, which leads to tension and conflict. As a teen you are searching for your place in the world in order to become your own person. Odd as it seems you also need the attachment to your mother to feel safe to go out on your own, the relationship becomes a juggling act. You are juggling two balls, the "I am not a baby anymore" ball and the "I do need you, but…." ball. As a young girl your mother had an answer for everything, her advice was like pearls strung gently around your heart. But lately, the pearls feel like bricks pressing down on your chest. You feel the urge to scream at the 2 hour lectures that were once 5 minutes. Instead of screaming you make facial expressions, or mumble under your breath which adds another 2 hours because she has to remind you of your attitude. While your mother is lecturing you are thinking of a way to get your point across without yet "another lecture," but once she gets on a roll, she keeps going like the "Energizer Bunny." As she talks you want to escape, but as you walk off, she follows you to your room and continues, her words now sounding like a blur. Does the scenario sound familiar? Many teens can relate, it's a common scene in many households. If you have a great relationship with your mother your days may be easier, but you have probably witnessed a mother-daughter stand off or heard your friends complain.

> "Having a great relationship with your mother plays a big role in a teen's life. Your mother is your confidant, your friend and your biggest cheerleader. The relationship I have with my mother has had a major impact in my life. My mother always makes it comfortable and is always very open to talk about anything I'm going through. She always motivates me to strive and be the best that I can be. Without her I don't know where I would be. A mother/daughter relationship is a strong bond that should never be broken." -Skylar T.

Even girls with great relationships with their mothers have situations and topics they feel uncomfortable talking to their mothers about. There are two reasons, one, they think their mother may get upset, two, they don't want their mothers to lose respect for them. When it comes to certain topics like, dating, curfews, extent of punishments, style of dress, and sexual relationships, it doesn't matter how close you are to your mother, those are topics that can cause a bit of hesitancy.

Many teens feel like their mothers think they know everything, their mothers feel like the teens don't know anything, which causes chaos. Life could be easier for you but realize, no matter how strong your argument is, you will never win, so in order to have a peaceful relationship, you may need to re-evaluate your actions. Of course you are smart and know some things, but you do not have the life experiences your mother has from her years on earth.

As a teen, my mother's lectures to my sister's and I would somehow include, "Two grown women cannot live under the same roof, so until you can take care of yourself and get your own house, I am the only woman in this house!" We would "think", (of course not say) "I can't wait to move out!" Have you ever felt that way?

Mother-daughter relationships are very complex; she is someone who you will idolize or resist. There are mother-daughter relationships where the mother is strictly the mother, nothing more, nothing less, no joking, playing around, or thinking about crossing the line. Mother-daughter relationships where the mother is more like a sister and the daughter has no restrictions, they wear one another's clothes, hang out at the same places, and get along…like sisters. Mother-daughter relationships that are so strained, even living in the same home, they never talk and can't seem to see eye to eye about anything, they do not agree on things as simple as the weather. Some teens want to be just like their mothers when they grow up and some want to be totally opposite. There has to be a balance in order for you and your mother to get along. As I said earlier, you will never win the debate, you have to take ownership of your feelings and try to understand your mothers perspective. Being a mother myself, I can speak for other mothers, we only want the best for our daughters. Mistakes we have made in life we want our daughters to avoid, therefore it gets frustrating if we feel we are not getting our point across.

It is possible to have a good relationship with your mother, but it starts with a change of your mindset, arguing, facial expressions, and pouting, is not the solution. There are ways for you to reduce the tension. Even if your relationship has been rocky, since you are going to be living there a few more years, it's not too late to make some changes. Being aware of your actions can prevent petty disagreements that turn into major battles. Now, change takes time and practice, you may read these suggestions and say, "That won't work with my mother!" Don't give up until you try…think positive!

When you and your mother are frustrated, both are responsible for your own actions, since you can't control her actions, you have to control yours.

Darolyn D. Mangum

> **Here's what you do:** remain calm, listen to what your mother is saying, avoid rude comments and facial expressions, and keep in mind, you need a place to stay. :) Again, it takes practice! Remember the saying, "When mama is happy, everybody is happy!" If you have a great relationship with your mother, cherish it!

My Jewelry Box

Chapter 4

"I'm a Teen Drama Queen!"

"I don't have haters, they are fans in denial"—Unknown

Does that title sound familiar? Does it sound like it could be a reality TV show? I am sure many of you are familiar with Love and Hip Hop, Bad Girls Club, Pretty Little Liars, Dance Moms, Keeping Up With the Kardashians, America's Next Top Model, Bring It, to name a few. Day or night you can find a reality show, it appears that a new one is aired every week. The unfortunate "reality" is that many teenage girls think these shows reflect real life and base their relationships and friendships around what they see. Is your attitude, beliefs, self-image, or behavior affected by what you watch on reality shows? Do you feel that reality TV represents real life?

Reality television can have a big influence and impact on your attitude. What you see is not necessarily the real lives of the people on the shows. The stars are paid to entertain, situations are set up, scenes are edited to make things seem more dramatic and exciting. If you notice there is always, a fight, or some kind of drama on most reality shows. Often teen females portray the attitudes of the women they see on tv because it's glamorized, they are sassy, arrogant, mean, bullies, fighters, or the busy body who's always in everybody's business. Our attitude determines how far we will go in life, so be sure if someone impresses you enough to mimic their attitude, be sure it's positive and ladylike.

As a teen, when I grew up we did not have reality TV shows, we had family based shows that taught life lessons; some that you may not have heard of. If you get a chance, Google the shows and watch a clip, look at the style of dress, hairstyles, conversations, attitudes, and the activities the teens engaged in. Our favorites were: The Brady Bunch, Family Affair, The Walton's, Happy Days, Different Strokes, I Love Lucy, All in the Family, Carol Burnett, Ed Sullivan, I Dream of Jeannie, Bewitched, The Beverly Hillbillies, Green Acres, Leave It To Beaver, Gilligan's Island, I could go on and on. Thinking about the shows makes me laugh and smile. There was no violence, cursing, aggressive behavior, or sexual behavior. There were conflicts and people got angry on the TV shows, but they were handled and resolved in respectful ways. Teens didn't talk back, rarely got punished, before the show would end, everyone was happy and ready to move on to the next venture. When the show would go off we would be thinking about the moral of the story, not thinking of negative, devious things to do.

When you watch the reality shows you can start believing things that are shown on TV that are not real or positive. Your beliefs and thoughts of yourself change because the influence is so realistic. The way the shows are set up, it seems there is no way it can be fake. The females fight and throw drinks on each other, the one that looks like the hero and won the fight is the one everyone talks about the next day… before you know it, there are imitators of her, or things she said. Some teens actually look for the baddest girl on the show, because she gets the most attention.

> "My parents don't like for me to watch reality shows. I like them because I can see the other side of life being rich and having fun. I would like to be an actress and be on a reality show. I love Bad Girls Club, my favorite actress of all times is Meghan James. She's pretty and I like her personality, plus she can fight. LOL! I love her!"- Alexis W.

Seeking attention changes your self-image. Some teens feel in order to get attention they have to change who they are. Reality shows are perfect to look for an image, it's like shopping at the personality store, there are so many personalities to choose from. You can find the sweet girl, bossy girl, pretty girl, physically fit girl, pretty hair girl, the messy girl, the quiet girl, they have all types of personalities. For teens who want to fit in and are seeking attention, there is also "peer pressure." When you hear a phrase like "peer pressure," you think about doing things influenced by friends or society like drugs and alcohol, sex, bullying, not focusing in school. Teen girls often face social pressure in one or more of these topics, but they should pressure each other to do things their parents would approve of, such as doing well in school and getting along with their family. Social pressure can cause problems for teen girls. In order to fit in they will idolize a popular reality star and do everything to imitate her. They will dress like her, talk like her, behave like her, and perfect her image. Once you try to be someone else it's difficult to be yourself because you feel that being you isn't good enough.

The females on the reality shows, wear designer clothes, sunglasses, shoes, purses, and jewelry, on top of living in a big, beautiful house with designer furniture, maids, chefs, nanny's, let's not forget the fancy cars, their perfect bodies, hair, nails, and makeup. What young girl wouldn't dream of having that life? There are adult women who desire the same things. The influence of the reality show stars can create low-self esteem which can cause you to think and feel unhappy about your body, lifestyle, and who you are. Reality TV is meant for entertainment, not transformation!

It's okay to be a "drama queen" if that's your real personality, but be original. Understanding how to be your original self begins with understanding who you are in the first place.

> **Tip:** Be real to yourself.... that's your reality!

My Jewelry Box

Darolyn D. Mangum

Chapter 5

Friends- How Many "Likes" Do You Have?

It's not how many friends you can count, it's how many of those you can count on. –Anthony Liccione

Middle and high school is usually the time when friendships change. Many teens who have been friends since kindergarten find themselves going their separate ways as they get into their teen years. Between the cliques, bullies, mean girls, and fake girls, knowing how to develop a healthy friendship can be a challenge. (Best Friends Forever) BFF's who you once thought of as an inseparable sister has suddenly become a frenemie (a friend who is now acting like an enemy). One important thing is although teens want to have friends and not be alone, be careful not to get caught up in wanting friends so badly that you get used and mistreated by others in order to be friends.

If someone doesn't want to be friends, don't force it, in the end, you will be the one to get your feelings hurt. It's better to have friends who want to be friends, rather than being with friends who don't want you around.

Friendship issues are common (and they don't go away completely when you become an adult), for most girls, middle school is the time when the friendship roller-coaster starts. Middle school can be uncomfortable and very awkward. Its seems like everything around you is changing: your relationship with your family, your body, your attitude, now on top of all of that, the person you share laughs with, talk to, and look forward to being with is also changing. You are beginning to wonder, "What have I done?" "Why are me and my childhood BFF arguing so much?" All of a sudden you realize what the word "drama" means. Every time you look around there is "drama" with close friends and other girls at school. Longtime friendships are falling apart left and right. It can be very hard to fix a broken friendship and it doesn't always make sense to try. The reality is that some friendships are not meant to last. Girls often feel secure with their own circle of friends sometimes called, "cliques," they can control who they are friends with, and who they choose not to be friends with. In the "cliques" there is usually one girl who controls who is a part of the group, she is considered the "ring leader," the bossy/mean girl, the girl who bullies other girls in the group. Bullies can either be bossy and just a lot of talk, or there are bullies who don't mind fighting and are physically and verbally abusive. There are bullies in most groups, even the "good" girls group has a leader or someone the other girls look up too. Good girl bullies are usually just bossy, they don't fight or verbally abuse, they just tell everybody what to do. Girls know who the bullies are, but they stay in the group for fear of being alone because they feel they will not fit in with other "cliques." However, human bullies still exist, cyber bullying is also becoming popular.

With the use of technology in today's society, friendship has taken on a new meaning for teens. The use of the cell phone, Internet, and social networking has changed the way friends connect and interact. Technology has created more weapons for teens to use that keep friction going between girls. Facebook, Twitter, Instagram, Snapchat, email, and texting are just some of the weapons used that are destroying friendships.

When I was a teen, friendships were much different. We would actually be with our friends, laugh, talk, and have person to person interaction. We couldn't wait for opportunities to go outside all day during the summer and after our homework was done on school days. We would go outside, play jacks, jump rope, hula hoop, hopscotch, skate, ride bikes, and enjoy our friends. (Yes, we played outside as teens.) We didn't have the distractions of cell phones, social media, or video games. Of course friendships would have issues, and yes, there was "drama" at school, but it was things like, girls writing notes about each other, or talking behind each other's back, there were physical fights, but usually within days the girls would become friends again. In today's society, teens resort to physical violence with weapons or destroying images through the use of technology. The disagreements we had as teens were nothing compared to the teens of today's society. Teens often focus on what can be done in order to permanently cause harm to someone's image.

In the world of technology at the click of a button, a rumor can spread, pictures can be shared, and other malicious or cruel things can be done. Within minutes the details of a conflict can end up in another state by use of the internet.

Teens focus on being popular in a different way today, they are concerned with how many friends they have and how many "likes" they can get on social media. Many of you have 700 friends on Facebook and feel like you are such a popular person. You post a picture and get 100's of likes, but your personality has you as one of the most disliked people at school. Social skills are limited due to social media and technology. No one has to talk if they choose not too, it's a matter of texting, in boxing, snap chatting, sending an email, and various other forms of technology. The odd thing is teens will decide not to talk to someone at school because they don't trust them, but they will reveal information about themselves and trust strangers they meet on social media.

There are things you should know about the dangers of befriending strangers on the internet, you must be wise: Be careful revealing personal information such as where you live, what school you attend, your daily whereabouts, and do not post inappropriate pictures or send them via text messaging/email.

Teens today rarely talk; actually, adults are falling into that mindset as well. I have seen teens and adults sit side by side and text rather than talk to one another. It is rare to go to the mall or other public places and not see people focusing on their cell phones rather than talking to one another. A group of teens can be together and every one of them has their head down, in deep thought on their phones. If you are not careful, they will bump into you because as they walk they are not paying attention to what's ahead, their focus is on what's in their hand. Even through formal writing, teens use social media slang (before-b4, on the way-OTW, LOL-Laugh out loud, idk- I don't know) because they text so much. If cell phone towers lost signal for a long period of time, teens would not know how to effectively communicate. Friendships are based on technology more than actual human contact.

TIP: As a teen do you know the true meaning of friendship, or do you consider a "clique" friendship? Are your social media friends considered your "true" friends, even though the only time you spend with them is online?

"Teen girls do value their friendships because they feel like having a close friend is important because they would be someone to confide in. Your friends may have similar issues and situations going on in life just like you. It's great to share fun experiences with your friends."-Cali C.

My Jewelry Box

_____

_____

_____

_____

_____

_____

_____

When you are happy, you enjoy the music. But, when you are sad, you understand the lyrics..

Chapter 6

Do You Hear What I Hear?

"Music is What Feelings Sound Like"–Unknown

Most of us absolutely love music. We are moved, inspired and connected by it. Music reflects something about who we are. If I asked you to tell me your favorite singers, groups, videos, or songs, most of you could quickly rattle off a list. Our favorite singers captivate us with words that have powerful messages and sounds that we can relate to in some type of way. Teens follow musicians through various forms of media and on the Internet, often spending more time studying artists lifestyles then they do their work for school. Most of you know more about Nicki Minaj, Taylor Swift, Beyonce, Drake, Chris Brown, Rhianna, One Direction, Aryana Grande, and Miley Cyrus then you do about the Texas History lesson you learned in class.

In fact, most of you probably have created playlists and haven't created a study guide for your next big test. Playlist are well thought out for almost every situation and emotion you may experience: a relaxed playlist for a "chilled" night at home; an upbeat playlist for workouts; a gloomy playlist for those low moments; and an angry playlist that says all the things you want to tell the person who made you upset.

Music can be a great way to express yourself and deal with challenging situations in life, sometimes life is just plain hard. It could be a conflict with your family, the end of a friendship or relationship. In these tough life moments, music can be a positive way to express who you are and what you are feeling. Whether you relate to rap, R & B, techno, country, or heavy metal, music is a way to express emotions.

However, you probably spend much of your free time listening to music. Music and its artists influence lifestyles of many of you. Teens idolize and imitate artists, especially because of the attention the artists receives in media. Great example, when Nicki Minaj became popular the female teen world went "pink." Most girls were in the world of Nicki Minaj, their hair, nails, makeup and the famous pink lipstick were all the rage.

Teen music choices also depend on your peers; friends play an important role in the habits you mimic from various musicians and music videos. Music plays an important role in shaping your ideas and interests. Music videos can sometimes influence teens to get interested in learning to play different instruments or learn the latest dance moves. However, the glamorous lives of pop musicians create unrealistic expectations and are far more interesting then the music itself. Most artist have lavish jewelry, fancy cars, big mansions, and lots of money. Even young artists have their own homes in which their parents live with them. They have chauffeurs or their parents drive their cars because they are not old enough to drive. You may develop musical interests for the wrong reasons. It is important that you understand the reality in the music industry. The music you listen to is likely to influence the choices you make. For example, songs with words that express violence will likely influence some teens to get violent because they think its cool. Teenagers who listen to music with the main message being sex or music with strong sexual language are more likely to dress more revealing and indulge in sex at an early age because of the curiosity of what the musicians are describing.

Pop music influences the fashion choices teenagers make. Musicians are trendsetters and are often featured in magazines, fashion blogs and various media that teenagers use for fashion inspiration. For instance, the clothes some females see the girls wear on music videos are tight, revealing and inappropriate to wear anywhere but the club, but teens think its ok to wear the clothes on an everyday basis. Teens often look up to these artists as cool and will often imitate their styles on the red carpet and in music videos. The pressure to look cool may affect many teenagers' self-esteem if they cannot afford the clothes everyone else wears. You should develop a personal sense of style and only rely on the music videos and artists as entertainment.

The media can certainly affect a teenager's self-image. Females who are sexy or beautiful in movies, on TV, or on other media platforms can influence teen girls to act and dress like them. Media descriptions of style, dating and sex can have a lingering effect on a teen's understanding of normal relationships, including sexual responsibility. The images of females in media can influence the way you view yourself and your body in a negative way. A controversial trend in which music affects style, especially in female teens, is the use of excessive make-up, hair extensions, fake lashes, and the new trend of enhanced rear ends. Just think before going to bed if girls, peel off layers make up, take out hair extensions, remove lashes, the image of that girl is laying on the dresser. She goes to bed as a different person, who wouldn't dare leave the house without looking camera ready. The influence of lyrics in songs and the images on videos, can affect decisions teens make and how they feel.

Parents and other trusted adults try to talk to teens by sharing their own values and the consequences they faced regarding irresponsibility. Even though consequences are shared some teens want to have their own experiences and thing adults don't understand because, "times are different." Indeed they are, teenagers have access to so many influences due to technology. For instance, growing up in the 70's we had a radio that was usually in a room of the home where the entire family could listen to it. We didn't have headphones, cell phones, iPods, etc. Plus, the lyrics of the music wasn't based on sexual and explicit language. Today, as teens you have access to music from your phones, internet, and friends, you do not depend on music your parents play in the car or the stereo at home. As a result, it is now more difficult to sensor the kind of music teens have access too. Some lyrics use inappropriate sexually explicit language and curse words that teens easily adopt because of the words and beat of the music. This affects your language in a negative way, especially if you begin to curse or use insulting words. On the flip side, music can influence teens in a positive way.

The kind of music you listen to can have a positive influence on you socially and mentally. Music can increase your mood; it helps you look at your life by looking at things happening in today's society. Although parents have a hard time seeing anything positive in the music today because many parents don't understand the language or dislike the words. Sadly, the words they do understand are inappropriate, so music you listen to doesn't have a chance with your parents because they think it's a bad influence. It's funny to hear teens explain the meaning of words in songs to their parents. Popular words are "bae"(baby or sweetie), "thirsty"(desperate), "On Fleek" (on point), "Turn Up" (get pumped up). Turn Up is an example of a phrase used from a song by artist, Lil Jon, "Turn Down For What."

> "My mom was going through the house singing and dancing to," Partition", by Beyonce' ,she was really into it, wrong words and all, until I asked if she knew what the song was about. Once I explained it, she had a blank stare on her face. It was hilarious. She loved the song because it was Beyonce'. Now she doesn't like it anymore. LOL"- Shannon P.

Music can improve moods, when you have a bad day at school, disagreements with your friends or parents, you can go to your room and turn on some music to calm down. You can listen to music at anytime on you smartphone, or listen to music on YouTube. Music is often the link between teens and a balanced social life. Your social life is an important part of who you are. You want to put your social skills to work by meeting and interacting with new people, and learning new ideas that are positive. If you are socially inactive, you should work on improving your social skills, get involved with people, try new things! Your musical influences are a way of better understanding who you are and what you are experiencing in your life.

> **TIP:** Your choice of music can be a reflection of your mood or personality; don't allow what you hear to make you who you are!

My Jewelry Box

Chapter 7

It's Not What You Wear It's How You Wear It!

"Style Is A Way To Say Who You Are Without Having To Speak."– Rachel Zoe

Parents and daughters have battled over what is "appropriate" and "not appropriate" dress for generations. I remember disagreeing with my mother over wearing something she felt was not appropriate for school. As a teen you feel as though your parents do not know the style and want you to look old fashioned. My sisters and I would always say, "Everybody wears this!" My mother would say, "Well you are not everybody else and everybody else is not my responsibility." Dressing with respect was a biggie in our home. We were taught that what you wear represents you because your reputation follows you throughout life. All households are different, we had friends growing up, who would wear God knows what to school and their parents dropped them off, so of course the parents saw their outfits before they left home! We would think, "Wow!" "They have nice parents!"

Times have surely changed. Some teens wear outfits to school that seem more appropriate for a hip hop video then a classroom. There are some who dress very casually and feel their attire is appropriate for any occasion.

> "Parents should not tell us what to wear to school. We know what we can wear, some kids wear things out of dress code and never get in trouble. Most of the time the administrators and teachers don't say anything."-Julie H.

Teen girls are dressing according to what's fashionable for their life's purpose. High school girls are usually focused on attracting boys, middle school girls are trying to fit in and impress their friends. For instance, skinny jeans, short skirts, cut-off shorts, etc. are not for everybody. Unfortunately, every style is not for every body type. Clothing makes a personal statement about teen girls. There's a difference between being cute or pretty and being provocative. Girls may be athletic, girly, nerdy or a tomboy. The clothes you wear express your personality and says a lot about you and the things you are interested in. Teens do not like parents telling them what they should or should not wear. If your parents told you what to wear every day, you would feel out of place. To wear clothes that are not your style would make you feel as if you were in someone else's body or playing a dress-up game. Fashion is all about self-expression, as a teen, dressing in your own style will make you feel confident in yourself; even if it is not acceptable to anyone else.

It's common for teens to shop in stores like Aeropostale, Charlotte Russe, Forever 21, Hollister and Abercrombie & Fitch, because teens today are very name brand conscience. Although, most of the clothing at these stores appear to be geared for the high school and college crowd, middle school girls can be found scanning the racks and purchasing outfits in those stores. The "Pink" collection at Victoria's Secret also attracts the teen market, although it is targeted for college students.

Appropriate attire for teens has changed so much, some girls don't realize their clothing may be considered inappropriate. Teens say they are only following fashion that is trendy. Girls, let me explain, showing bra straps, wearing extra tight tank tops, skirts and shorts that barely touch the tops of your thighs, that are so short if you bend over you will see your underwear, that is not appropriate. You should focus on creating a positive image of respect and representing who you are. If you want to be known as a respectful young lady, pay attention to what you wear. A good rule of thumb is, "if you can't bend over without showing your underwear it's too short, if every curve, roll, or print of your bra or panties are showing, it's too tight, If you bend forward and the person in front of you can see your breast, your shirt is too low."

Wearing your best clothing and accessories is important to teenage girls. Middle school and high school years are a time of trying to fit in while still trying to find out who you are. Fashion is very important to teen self-esteem, looking attractive and wearing clothes that make you look good will help you feel good about yourself and your appearance. The right clothing is important, even the right makeup, shoes and accessories. A young girl who is forced to wear hand-me-downs from older siblings will not feel as confident as a teen who wears new or trendy fashions to school on a regular basis. Also, a teen whose parents can't afford to buy clothes in current styles may feel awkward, as though every one is staring at them. However, there are some teens so academically focused, they are confident in who they are, they do not get concerned if they are not dressed trendy.

What you wear often identifies you as belonging to specific cliques or groups who wear similar clothing. For instance, some girls only wear name brand clothing and shoes, if you notice, so does all of their friends. There are the girls who wear all black, some dress like grown women, some dress like athletes…notice, so do the girls they hang with. It gives teens a sense of belonging and togetherness (being with your friends who have similar interest in style raises levels of confidence

Pearls 4 Girls

and builds some teen's self-esteem). If you notice, in today's society, you rarely see an unfashionably dressed student with a group of students who are dressed in designer attire. As a teen, my parents could not afford and did not believe that name brand clothes was priority over academics, therefore I wore what they could afford which wasn't name brand. Some of my friends, on the other hand, wore name brand clothes which I would have loved to wear. Even though I was always neat, my clothing matched and I was clean, I hung out with the trendy , name brand wearing students because I had confidence. My clothes did not make me who I was. When around my friends, I felt that my clothes were just as nice as theirs and I looked just as pretty, I had my own style.

To some teens, friends are important and wearing clothes similar, makes you feel equal in your group. Most girls use their clothes, accessories and fashion to define who they are, make statements about their choice of friends, and establishes their identity.

> **TIP**: If you want to make a statement of who you are by your clothing, this is the statement you should make…without saying a word, your look should say, "I AM A RESPECTFUL YOUNG LADY! MY BODY IS FOR ME TO SEE! I AM NOT AN ADVERTISEMENT FOR CLOTHING COMPANIES; I DO NOT HAVE TO FOLLOW TRENDS TO KEEP FRIENDS!"

Darolyn D. Mangum

My Jewelry Box

Chapter 8

I've Got Manners, How About You?

"Good Manners and Kindness are Always in Fashion"—Unknown

Good manners never go out of style, they are a plus for any teenager. Manners begin in your early years, they are taught and influenced by your environment and the people you are around. Role models and practice are the most effective ways to teach good manners. When I grew up teens were stressed the importance of manners. For instance, we could not talk, interrupt, or be in the presence of adults while they were having a conversation, there was no whispering around others, it was a "must" to clean up behind yourself. There were many rules that were stressed. Here are some basic manners you can start practicing now:

Manners Toward Parents (or any adult)

- Show respect by your words, body language and

attitude.

- Talk in a reasonable tone and volume.

- Take responsibility for your behavior, accept the consequences of misbehavior, and apologize for the disobedience.

Manners Towards Siblings

- Siblings can be pests, but don't be rude, or unkind.

- Apologize when you are wrong and look for ways to make things right.

- Respect your sibling's property.

- Always practice being a role model to younger siblings.

Manners Outside the Home

- Treat everyone as you want to be treated.

- Use the same manners outside the home as you do at home.

- Speak respectfully to everyone, being honest and courteous.

- If you do not use inappropriate language at home, don't use it away from home.

-

General Manners & Kindness

- Turn off what you turn on, close what you open, clean up what you mess up.

- Give your seat to an older adult or mom with a baby, hold the door for someone who has their hands full.

- Say, "please" and "thank you" when necessary.

- Good manners mean showing kindness and respect to others. If someone falls, you should ask, "Are you OK? Can I help you?"

-

Social Manners

- Blowing your nose discreetly and not at the dinner table.

- Sneeze into your elbow

- Say "excuse me" after passing gas or burping in the presence of others.

- Speaking quietly indoors

- Hold the door open for others as they approach.

Growing up can be challenging for girls because the expectations to always exhibit manners are higher than for boys. Although, times have changed, girls have the same opportunities as boys. You may one day, be active in politics, or a CEO of a company. It is important for you to have the social tools you will need as you get ready for adulthood. Practice makes perfect!

1. Dress with respect. Clothes that are too tight, too low or too revealing sends the wrong message for females at any age. Just because it is in the stores or in the magazines does not mean it is appropriate.

2. Learn that you do not have to accept "No" as an answer. If you want something in life and it is not available the first time, continue to work for it, research, study and persevere. Don't give up and don't settle.

3. Choose friends that share your same values.

4. You do not have to be close friends with everyone.

5. Always be the one others can trust.

6. Be a good friend by not gossiping when told something in confidence.

7. Avoid using bad language, even if others are doing so.

8. Be a good sport – both when you lose and when you win.

9. Pay attention to how you speak. Replace "hafta" with "have to," "doncha" with "don't you," "gonna" with "going to," etc.

10. Be a good listener, don't talk while others are talking.

Cell Phone Manners

1. Restaurants: Put your phone on vibrate to prevent unnecessary noise if your cell phone rings. Only make outgoing calls if necessary and keep them brief. When people call you, let them know that you are eating.

2. Movies, Theaters, and Plays: Turn your phone off before you enter the venue.

3. Churches, Synagogues, and Other Places of Worship: Turn your phone off or leave it in the car. You and everyone around you should be able to worship in peace.

4. In the Checkout Line: If you are standing in the

checkout line, talking on a cell phone is rude to everyone around you—from the other customers in line to the cashier. You can wait a few minutes to talk on the phone. Don't initiate a call while standing in line. If the phone rings and you feel that you must answer it, let the person know you'll call right back.

5. Private Talk: When you're hanging out with friends and family, don't be rude and talk with someone else on your cell phone.

6. Texting: Avoid texting while you are engaged in an activity or meal with someone else. Texting in front of others is like whispering behind someone's back.

> "I get upset when my parents take my phone for punishment, they think every little thing I do means taking my phone away. It really irritates me because it makes no sense at all."-Melody A.

> **TIP**: Manners are things we do on a regular basis, but we are not good at them unless we practice, always remember…MIND YOUR MANNERS! A girl with good manners will always stand out in a crowd.

My Jewelry Box

DARE 2 DREAM!

Gymnast, Ahnyah Arie Durand, 6th grade student,

from Texas, is a true example of a teen accomplishing her dreams, by hard work and dedication. She began to show interest at the age of 7 and trains at Sonic Cheer/Omni Athletics. She is coached by Coach Calvin Parker and spends approximately 17hours per week at the gym. Several of her accomplishments include the following:

2013 National Gold Medalist-Double Mini Trampoline Level 6

2014 National Bronze Medalist - Double Mini Trampoline Level 7

2014 Regionals - Trampoline 6th out of 47

2014 State- 4th place double mini, second place trampoline

2014 State Champion on floor (3rd Place all around)

2014 Houston National Invitational - 3rd place floor/1st level 7 trampoline/1st level 7 double mini

Ahnyah has a host of spectators and a great fan base. Her grandmother, Rhonda Durand and aunt, Alexis Durand, who is also a cheer and tumbling coach at Sonic Cheer/Omni Athletics are big influences in her life.

Her goals for the future are to participate in, "Worlds for Cheer" and to go to the U.S. Olympics and have her name amongst the great Olympians, Gabi Butler and Gabby Douglas.

Chapter 9

Journaling Dreams, Thoughts, and Affirmations

"Goals May Give You Focus, But Dreams Give Power"—John Maxwell

As you go through life on your personal treasure hunt, in order to fill your treasure chest with life's precious memories, you must have an idea of your goals to know what you are "searching" for. Setting goals and having dreams is an exciting part of growing up and planning for your future. We all know that our imagination can take us places, our thoughts are unlimited! I am sure you daydream and imagine being someplace special, having a certain something you've always wanted, or meeting someone you've always wanted to meet. As a teen, it is very common when things happen in life to say, "I wish I….!" You can end that sentence with so many things. Dreams get more detailed as you get older, because you have experiences to increase your imagination. To make your dreams a reality takes work and lots of positive thinking. Once you learn how to put your dreams into goals, and take action, you can create your path to success!

Little girls imagine and dream of being a princess with a pretty pink dress, beautiful shoes, a shiny tiara, living in her beautiful castle. Teenage girls daydream about shopping sprees, that cute boy "Isaac" in Science class, her shiny new car, parents that let her make her own decisions, how her life will be when she is out of her parents house, and life without punishment. It doesn't stop as a teen, adults dream too! We dream of being rich, having children who listen, a big fancy house, expensive clothes, expensive jewelry, multiple garages with your dream cars in each one, a paradise vacation, and the list goes on. Notice how the older you get the longer your list gets? It's a nice get away to daydream about happy thoughts when life gets in the way, we all need a mental escape. Finding your personal happy place is a must in order to get out of moods that can ruin a moment or your entire day.

To find your happy place you must focus on dreams and goals that you want to come true. For instance, picture a life that would make you happy: what kind of family would you have, where would you live, how would you dress, what career would you have, who would you spend time with, what places would you like to visit, etc.? Once you find your happy place, you have to have a plan. How can you make this come true? Are there things you can do now to reach some of your goals? Can you do some things now to make life at home easier? Are there things you can do to get closer to your career goals? Your desires are actually goals for your future! Believe and you can achieve! I am sure you have heard that before.

Do you have a dream or a vision for your life already? Have you thought about what you want and how you can achieve it? To not have a vision, dream, or goal is like getting on a plane with no destination, just flying among the clouds going wherever the clouds take you. Setting goals puts you in control, you choose where you want to go and what it takes to get there.

One great way to focus on your goals is journaling. Journaling is a way for you to write down your feelings, goals, write steps to achieve your goals, and help you stay focused. Journaling is also a way to help you understand yourself better, it is also a form of personal expression. A journal is a safe place to be yourself; to feel, think, express, and dream. You can write in a tablet, a journal, use a spiral tablet, or create your own. Its purpose is to also help you to use your imagination and improve communication skills. There are times when you are happy, sad, angry, depressed, or you may just want to write thoughts and feelings that you may not want to express to others.

Journaling can help you at home, at school, while traveling, etc. During difficult times, such as being upset, concerns with grade changes, injury, addition of a new family member, or loss of a loved one. These events often cause strong feelings, such as emotional pain, confusion, insecurity, anger, fear, sadness or grief. Journaling can be used as a "good friend," it's a place for you to express difficult feelings. Sometimes it is hard to put feelings into words, so drawing, writing, or even scribbling can be a good way to let those feelings out. There are times, you may need to talk, but there is no one around to talk to. At that time your journal becomes a way to express your feelings without being blamed or judged. Journaling is not to keep secrets from your parents or to write things that you may need to seek adult or professional help with.

Use journaling as a way to be creative. Many musicians, poets, and writers started their careers simply by keeping a journal of their thoughts and feelings. Songs and poetry are feelings that are expressed in writing. It is suggested to journal in a comfortable, relaxing and quiet place, free from interruptions and distractions, so your creativity can flow. Each journal entry should be dated for you to keep track of events and things you want to refer to in the future.

> "I have a journal that I write in daily; it helps me to express my feelings and emotions. Sometimes I feel much better about situations after I write."-Ling N.

Another form of journaling is writing affirmations. Affirmations are positive statements about who you are and what you can become. They help you focus on what you want. Affirmations really work, by helping you focus on positive things. You should write your affirmations and say them when you wake up, throughout the day, or as often as you want. Whenever you start to think negative thoughts about yourself or a situation. Saying something positive will help you to think better thoughts. You can write positive thoughts on a post it note, on your computer, on your notebook cover, or anywhere in your room to remind you to think positive. You can use your journal writing for affirmations, by writing positive things throughout the day can help you reach your goals.

Being a teenager can be a challenging time in life. Positive affirmations can help you focus on things that will help you reach your goals, develop confidence, and make you feel good about yourself. Even if initially you don't feel positive, keep saying the affirmations until they start feeling real and you start believing them.

Here are some examples of some affirmations or positive thoughts:

1. I am a happy, beautiful, positive, person.
2. I am a unique and priceless person.
3. I am a well liked person.
4. I am successful in everything I do and say.
5. I am creative, intelligent, attractive, energetic, witty, smart, healthy, wealthy, and wise.
6. I am a self determined person.
7. I love myself unconditionally just as I am.

It's easy to create your own to make them more personal for you. Here's how:

CREATING YOUR OWN AFFIRMATIONS

Affirmations should be stated in a positive way. For example, "I am happy." Instead of, "I am not sad." Affirmations should focus on what you want, stay away from the word "not" in your affirmations. The words, "I AM" are powerful. You can add any positive words after I AM as your affirmation. I am beautiful, I am creative, I am smart, etc. Now you think of 3 to write in your journal. I am……. I am…….. I am……..

For example, "I am a cheerleader," instead of "I will be a cheerleader." Keep affirmations short and simple. When you write your affirmations, write them as if they already exist.

Dreams, goals, and affirmations are ways to set your sights on your future. You must focus on being positive and thinking positive thoughts.

> **TIP**: Keeping track of your dreams and affirmations will help you visualize where you are headed. You will have a destination because your journal will be your guide! Who is responsible for you accomplishing your dreams? Say it loud and proud…."I AM!"

My Jewelry Box

_____

_____

_____

_____

_____

_____

_____

Chapters 10

Keys to My Treasure Chest

"Life is a Treasure Chest Worth More than Gold"-Unknown

Chapters 1-9 contained the various gems in your jewelry box, this section is a guide and the key to open your treasure chest. You will discover many of the answers to finding your happiness as a teenage girl. The questions are from the previous chapters, take your time and think about your answers. I suggest you use a journal to answer the questions, be sure to date the entry. In a few months I would like for you to read the questions again and compare your answers, you should notice a change in your answers, because your attitude and mindset has changed.

Chapter 1-Free to Be Me

Do you struggle with your identity? If so, why?

_____

_____

Do you consider yourself having high or low self esteem? Why?

What is the thing you like most about who you are? What would you like to change, what steps do you need to take in order to change?

_____

_____

_____

_____

_____

Do you have an idol? If so, who and why is this person your idol?

_____

_____

_____

_____

_____

Chapter 2-Uniquely Me

What are your thoughts when you look in the mirror? Why?

_____

_____

_____

_____

_____

What do you like most when you look in the mirror? Why?

_____

_____

_____

_____

What do you like least when you look in the mirror? Why?

Chapter 3- Mothers vs. Daughters

What kind of relationship do you have with your mother? Describe how it makes you feel?

Are you happy with your relationship? If so, what makes you happy with the relationship? If not, why are you not happy?

Even if you have a great relationship with your mother, what would you like to see to make it even better?

Is there a mother/daughter relationship that you admire? What do you admire about it?

Chapter 4-"I'm a Teen Drama Queen!"

Do you watch reality TV shows? If so, what's your favorite one? What do you like most about it?

_____

_____

_____

_____

_____

Are you influenced by reality TV show stars? If so, what influences you, if not, why?

_____

_____

_____

_____

_____

Darolyn D. Mangum

If you could play a role in a reality show, would you? Why/Why Not?

___

Do you think reality shows are real or staged? Why?

Chapter 5- Friendships, How Many "Like" Do You Have?

What is your definition of friendship?

_____

_____

_____

_____

_____

_____

What qualities do you look for in a friend? What qualities do you have that makes you a good friend?

_____

_____

_____

_____

_____

Are you a part of a "clique" or would you rather be alone? Why?

_____

_____

_____

_____

_____

Chapter 6- Do You Hear What I Hear?

What's your favorite musical artist? Why?

_____

_____

_____

_____

_____

_____

What's your favorite song? Why?

_____

_____

_____

_____

_____

Do you listen to music when you are happy, sad, mad, or depressed? How does music affect how you feel?

_____

_____

_____

Does music make you feel better? If so, how, if not, why?

Do the words in songs influence the way you feel? Why/Why not?

_____

_____

_____

Chapter 7- It's Not What You Wear, It's How You Wear It

Do you follow trends from magazines, movies, or your friends regarding the clothes you wear? Why are trends important? If not, what is your personal style?

_____

_____

_____

_____

_____

_____

_____

When you get dressed, do you look at the image you are representing? Why is it important?

_____

_____

_____

_____

_____

_____

Do you think it's okay to wear shirts, skirts, or any clothing that shows excess skin? Why/Why not?

_____

_____

_____

_____

_____

_____

Chapter 8- I've Got Manners, How About You

Do you think manners are important? Why/Why not?

Do you act one way in front of adults and another way in front of your friends? Why can't you be yourself at all times?

_____

_____

_____

Are there any manners that you have been taught, that you don't think are necessary? Why/Why Not?

_____

_____

_____

_____

_____

Chapter 9 Journaling, Dreams, Goals & Affirmations

Do you have dreams for your future? What are they?

_____

_____

What are you goals? Academic, Career, and Personal?

Are you making plans to achieve your goals? What are you doing to work toward your goals?

_____

_____

_____

_____

_____

Do you think affirmations are important? Why/Why Not?

_____

_____

_____

_____

_____

_____

Now that you have answered the questions, you have treasures which are answers to put in your treasure chest. When you want to check your progress, go back and read the answers to your questions any time you are ready. Pay attention to how your answers have changed.

> **TIP**: Use your journal to record your daily thoughts, feelings, progress, and moods. Enjoy your treasures as a teen. Your pearls will be an important part of your journey. Grow in grace! You are a pearl now, as you get older…a diamond you will be!

Dare 2 Dream!!!

Conclusion

Darolyn's passion for empowering teens motivated her in January 2015, to launch a group for girls 6th-12th grade, "Teens with Dreams. "The mission is to allow girls to realize their dreams and goals are achievable. The group meets monthly for girls to interact encouraging social skills, share ideas, discuss issues related to self-esteem, peer pressure, social media influence, and various topics middle and high school girls are faced with. Role playing, games, guest speakers, and written activities are incorporated in discussions to engage them. It's a time to interact the "old fashioned" way, just good face to face interaction.

From the first session the question was asked, "Why can't we do this every Saturday, or more often than once a month, this is fun?" It is very satisfying to know my passion is being fulfilled by the positive responses from the teens.

"Teens with Dreams" has been such an inspiration parents have requested a group for 2nd-5th grade girls. The request was honored, "Denim and Pearls" was launched in February, 2015.

The feedback has been incredible! The teens are excited and motivated!

"Teens with Dreams is like a second home for me. It's like my safe place, somewhere I can go to just kick back and let loose. A place where I can express myself without being judged. I think it's great being able to talk to successful women about things that are going on in the world regarding young girls."-Moriah L.

"Teens with Dreams is a happy place where you can be yourself and not be judged. All of the girls in the group are like planted flower seeds who have dreams to pop right out and turn into strong beautiful flowers, but we need help reaching our dreams and that's why we have Ms. D to guide our growth as teens with dreams." -Ayanna R.

"Teens with Dreams has been something that has impacted my life in so many ways, simply because of the positivity and all the love the girls receive from Ms. Dee Dee. This lady has an impact on every person that walks through that door...not only is she a mentor, but Ms. Dee Dee is my second mother. When I'm around her all my worries and stress go away, she teaches us basics and the

fundamentals of life, what it's like to be a young woman growing up in society. She gives us something that no other human being could offer. I remember the 1st day I met her I felt like I was at home. Her pretty red cheeks continued to blush and her beautiful smile continued to show, making every individual feel a sense of welcoming. I remember the first day she had us make what she calls a "dream board" and on this board we were free to be us and put anything we wanted to strive for. With this board it gives us a desire because everyday we're looking at our dreams and what we want to become. She always tells us, "be the best we can be" no matter the circumstances and struggles, as teens we have to crawl before we walk and throughout life we're going to face obstacles and journeys, but when that time comes not only me, but all the girls can count on Mrs. Dee Dee.
- Victoria F.

"Teens with Dreams is like my second family. We share a bond bigger than most families. It helps us conduct ourselves as the beautiful young ladies we are. There is never a time where you feel out of place or not welcomed."- Skylar T.

Pearls 4 Girls

Teens with Dreams

Launched "Denim & Pearls" (2nd-5th grade) February 2015

www.ingramcontent.com/pod-product-compliance
Lightning Source LLC
Chambersburg PA
CBHW042340150426
43196CB00001B/8